My Sister, the Superstar

Story by Pamela Rushby

Illustrations by Claudio Cerri

Nelson

My Sister, the Superstar

Text: Pamela Rushby
Publishers: Tania Mazzeo and Eliza Webb
Series consultant: Amanda Sutera
  Hands on Heads Consulting
Editor: Gemma Smith
Project editor: Annabel Smith
Designer: Jess Kelly
Project designer: Danielle Maccarone
Illustrations: Claudio Cerri
Production controller: Renee Tome

NovaStar

ISBN 978 0 17 033400 6

Cengage Learning Australia
Level 5, 80 Dorcas Street
Southbank VIC 3006 Australia
Phone: 1300 790 853
Email: aust.nelsonprimary@cengage.com

For learning solutions, visit **cengage.com.au**

Printed in China by 1010 Printing International Ltd
1 2 3 4 5 6 7 28 27 26 25 24

*Nelson acknowledges the Traditional Owners and Custodians
of the lands of all First Nations Peoples. We pay respect
to Elders past and present, and extend that respect to
all First Nations Peoples today.*

Contents

Chapter 1

Never as Good

I'm Alice. I'm nine years old.
I have a little sister, Lily. Lily is eight.

Some kids think it's great to have a little
sister. Well, I do too – most of the time.
But sometimes, it's not great at all. Because
although she's younger than me, Lily is
better at some things than I am. In fact,
Lily is better at a whole *lot* of things.

Like last month, when there were try-outs for the school band. Our music teacher said Lily was good at keeping a beat. I was given a shaker. Lily is now learning to play the drums.

We both joined our local soccer team last year. Before long, Lily became the star striker. I spent a lot of time on the bench.

Mum and Dad always say to me, "You did your best, Alice. We're proud of you!"

The thing is, I *do* try my best, but I feel like I'm never as good as Lily.

Also, everybody seems to know who Lily is. As soon as she appears anywhere, people smile cheerfully and welcome her. "Hi, Lily!" they say. Then they look at me, smile politely and ask, "And who are you?"

I know I shouldn't be jealous of my little sister, but sometimes I feel ... *unhappy.*

Chapter 2

The Reader's Cup

The only place where everyone knows *me* is our local library. I read a lot, and I borrow books every week.

One day last month, Lily came to the library with me. As usual, the librarians waved to me and said, "Hi, Alice!"

Then Jamil, one of the librarians, smiled politely at Lily and said, "And who are you?" Usually, it was the other way around!

As I checked out my books, I noticed
a digital display near the counter.
It said, READER'S CUP. It was a reading
competition for kids.

Teams of kids had one month to read all
four books. At the end of the month,
the teams would compete in a quiz.

I was excited to see that one of the books was *Alice's Adventures in Wonderland* – one of my favourites!

"The quiz is online," Jamil explained. "So, on the day, teams log in from everywhere. There are even prizes."

"I'd love to be on a team!" I said.

"I thought you would," Jamil said. "This is perfect for you, Alice!"

And that made me feel really good.

Chapter 3

Both on the Team

A minute later, I didn't feel quite so good.

"Can I be on the quiz team, too?"
said a voice from beside me. It was Lily.

"Of course you can be on the team!"
said Jamil.

On the way home, I tried to talk Lily out of entering the Reader's Cup. I wanted this to be *my* thing – not something that Lily turned out to be the best at. *Again.*

"You have to read four books very carefully," I said to Lily. "You're too busy for that."

"I can do it," said Lily.

I was sure she could. And she'd probably do it better than me.

Over the next few days, I kept thinking about ways I could get Lily to forget about the Reader's Cup. I even thought about hiding the books, so she wouldn't be able to read them in time. But I decided I just couldn't do that.

So, over the next four weeks, we both read all the books.

Chapter 4

Who Are You?

On the day of the Reader's Cup quiz, Lily and I met our team at the library, ready to log in.

"Hooray, Alice is here!" Jamil called.

That made me feel good.

But then the quiz started, and Lily answered *a lot* of questions correctly. The other people in our team looked at each another in amazement.

I could feel myself growing quieter and quieter. This wasn't meant to happen! I was meant to be the best, this time.

The quiz was nearly over. The scores were level between our team and another one. It was down to the last question. We all listened carefully to the quizmaster onscreen.

"In the book *Alice's Adventures in Wonderland*, Alice meets a gigantic caterpillar sitting on a mushroom. What does the caterpillar say to Alice?"

"Come on, Lily!" everyone on our team said.
"What's the answer?"

But Lily didn't know. And no one else did,
either.

I should know this, I thought to myself, anxiously. *I've read that book so many times! What does that caterpillar say?*

Words were rattling around in my mind. They were words that people often said to me. *Who are you? Who are you ...? Who ... are ... you?*

That was the answer! "It's 'Who are you?'"
I said.

And I was right! Our team won!

Everybody congratulated me – Lily more than anyone else. "You're the best, Alice!" she said.

I beamed. Because, just for once, I *was* the best at something. I knew what it felt like to be Lily, my superstar sister. And it felt great!